To

Robyn Heyder,

From the Oma

Margarethe Hildebrandt.

Date

Dezember 24. 1997.

HOLY
BIBLE

PRECIOUS MOMENTS™

Goodnight Book

PRECIOUS MOMENTS™

Goodnight Book

Stories and Prayers

Samuel J. Butcher, Illustrator
Betty De Vries, Compiler

BakerBooks
A Division of Baker Book House Co
Grand Rapids, Michigan 49516

Printed in the United States of America

Library of Congress Cataloging-in-Publication Data

Stories and Prayers / Samuel J. Butcher, illustrator : Betty De Vries, compiler.
p. cm. — (Goodnight book)
Summary: Each story in this collection focuses on a value or event familiar to the young child and closes with a prayer that can be said with the help of an adult.
ISBN 0-8010-4233-X
1. Children—Religious life. 2. Prayers—Juvenile literature. 3. Christian life—Juvenile literature. [1. Prayers. 2. Christian life.] I. Butcher, Samuel J. (Samuel John), 1939– ill. II. De Vries, Betty. III. Series: Goodnight book (Grand Rapids, Mich.) : 1.
BV4571.2.S74 1996
249—dc20 96-7360

Contents

Preface

There's something special about a favorite book for reading when a child is ready to be tucked in for the night. And when the stories focus on familiar values and everyday events, children want to hear them again and again.

These stories, written by several master storytellers, wear well and can be read and re-read without boredom. Child and adult can talk about the events and behavior patterns. Several stories close with an appropriate prayer that child and adult can say together.

The vocabulary is simple—designed to be read aloud to four-year-olds. Early readers will soon be reading favorite stories for themselves with only occasional help from an adult.

Sam Butcher's unique *Precious Moments* drawings with the large expressive eyes quickly convey joy, sadness, or humor. The soft, appealing colors attract both children and adults.

So the next time you hear, "I'm ready for a story now," pick up this happy combination of stories, prayers, and art. You and your child will not only be enjoying some very special minutes together, you will also be building some precious memories.

The Publishers

You and Yourself

Strong Muscles

One day Farmer John gave his son Joshua a small pig. It weighed only ten pounds. Each day Josh lifted the pig from one side of the fence to the other side so he could more easily clean its pen. As time passed the pig grew. Every day the pig

weighed just a little more. The day came when Josh could no longer lift the pig over the fence, but the daily exercise had made Josh's muscles much stronger than when he first began.

Have you ever watched a weight-lifting contest? Did you wish your muscles were as strong and big as those of the weight lifters?

Do you have a set of weights? If you would like to make a set, begin with a wooden broom handle or a piece of a metal pole and a little sand in a bag that you can put in two one-gallon pails or buckets. Put a bucket on each end of the pole. Pick up the pole and buckets and try to raise the pole to your shoulders. Keep adding sand as your muscles develop. One thing is certain, however; lifting the weights will do

you no good unless you lift them almost every day.

Learning to live for Jesus takes daily exercise too. Each time you make a decision to tell the truth and to be honest, your spiritual muscles grow stronger. Think about a way to live for Jesus and then be sure to do it tomorrow.

O Lord—I have
promised to obey your words.
Psalm 119:57

William C. Hendricks, adapted

By Name

What's your name? Matt? Kaitlyn? Jeremy? Ashley? Scott? Stephanie? Whether you like it or not, your name is one of the most interesting words you ever hear. You listen when you hear it. It spins you around, doesn't it?

Long ago, when God wanted to get Samuel's attention, he called him by name. The Bible tells us that "Samuel did not yet know the Lord." But the Lord knew him.

God knows your name too. He knows all about you. He knows what your weak

spots are. He knows your strong points too. Does that frighten you? It should make you happy that God knows all about you because he can also give you everything you need.

Listen for God. When God calls you, answer him, "Here I am, God. Use me. I'm ready to do what you want me to do." God can use even young children. He wants us to pray to him, to praise him. He also wants us to be happy and cheerful and honest. Sometimes those things are hard to do but God will help you if you ask him.

Speak, LORD, for your servant
is listening.
1 Samuel 3:9

Paul Martin, adapted

SamB

Yes and No

Yes and no are two of the smallest words in the English language. But they are probably the most important words in any language. When you were very small, these two words were among the first ones you learned to say.

Young children go through a stage when they say *no* to everything: "No, I don't want my milk." "No, I don't like potatoes." "No, I don't want to go to bed." "No, I won't stop banging my block on the table leg."

A child's *no* must be gradually changed to *yes* if he or she is to be a happy member of the family. Children have to learn when to say *no* and when to say *yes*.

It isn't just young children who have to learn this important lesson. All children and grown-ups have to learn it too. *No* is such a little word—it is easy to spell, it is easy to write, and it is easy to understand. But why is it so hard to use? When you play with your friends, will you be able to use this little word when you should?

When someone suggests that you play a mean trick on a friend, will you be able to say, "No, I will not do that!"

Sometimes *yes* is almost as hard to say as *no.* If you are asked about something wrong you have done, are you brave enough to say, "Yes, I did it"? Are you

brave enough to stand up to others and say, “Yes, I am a Christian,” or “Yes, I love Jesus”? Think about these words:

N-O is just a little word,
And so is Y-E-S.
But, oh, the difference they make,
No one could ever guess.
Say “N-O” to everything that’s wrong,
And “Y-E-S” to everything that’s right,
The whole day long.

Dena Korfker

Smiles of Joy

Look at your face in a mirror. Do you look happy or sad? It takes more muscles to look sad than to smile. When you wear a smile, it shines out to brighten the lives of everyone you meet.

If an apple is half ripe, one child may

say that it is half red already; another may say it is half green. If the lawn is half cut, one boy may say, "I'm half finished." Another boy may grumble, "I still have half to mow!"

Looking at the dark side can be a habit. Looking at the bright side can be a habit too.

The Bible tells Christians to be joyful—when we have little or when we have much; when we are sick or when we are well—even when we are punished for something we didn't do.

This is a good prayer to pray when you are ready to end the day:

Good night, Lord,
Thank you for the beautiful day.
Thank you for loving me.
Thank you for saving me.

Make me glad, not sad.
Help me to share my gladness
and my joy
With my friends, my family,
With everyone I meet tomorrow.
Good night, Lord,
Thank you for watching over me
while I sleep tonight.

A happy heart makes the face cheerful.
Proverbs 15:13

William C. Hendricks

You and Your Family

SamB

Mother

When you were a baby, one of the first words you learned to say was *mama,* or *mother. Mama* is the easiest word for a baby to say, and it's the word babies want to say most often. No one is as close to you as your mother. Before you were born you

were a part of your mother. No wonder babies want to be close to their mothers. Babies feel best when their mothers have their arms around them, hugging them tight.

And when you began to grow and were no longer a baby, who took your hand and helped you to walk? Who fed you your food until you learned to feed yourself? Who took care of you every day? Your mother! Why do you suppose mothers are willing to spend so much time with their children? Why are mothers so worried about what happens to their children? Why? Because that's what it means to be a mother! That's what a mother is. That's what a mother does.

Most children, especially if they are Christian children, never forget their

mothers, even when they are grown up and have become mothers and fathers themselves. They come back home again and again to visit their mothers. They show her how thankful they are for all she has done for them.

Five girls in the contest for a Miss Universe were asked, "If you could choose to be someone else, whom would you choose to be?" One of them said, "My mother! She is the most wonderful woman in the world."

Give your mother a hug today to show that you love her.

Honor your father and your mother.
Exodus 20:12

Dena Korfker, adapted

A New Baby

Tim looked at the funny little red-faced baby lying in the big basket that was all full of soft blankets. "Is *that* my new brother?" he asked. "Why doesn't he look at me? I'm his big brother."

Daddy and Mother both put their arms

around Tim and gave him a special "double hug." "Oooomph!" he grunted. "You're squashing me."

Daddy looked at the baby. "He's asleep, Tim. But even when he wakes up, it will be a while before he will want to look at anything except something to eat! He won't be able to see who you are until he grows up a little more. Then he'll be proud as proud can be to know that *you* are his big brother. He's a lucky baby!"

"Did I ever look like that?" asked Tim.

"You certainly did," said Mother. "Bring me the book of pictures from the shelf over there, and I'll show you how you looked the day you came home from the hospital."

Tim looked at the picture his mother showed him. "Did you love me when I

looked like that?" he asked. "I looked funny!"

Father sat down and Tim climbed up on his lap. "Big brother Tim," said Father, "we loved you then—all red and wrinkled up. We love you now—all strong and good-looking. We love Baby Sam just the way he is right now, and we love you just the way you are right now."

"Do I get half as much love now?" asked Tim. "There are two instead of one."

Mother smiled. "That's the best thing about love, Tim," she said. "There's no end to it. You don't have to divide it up, a bit here and a bit there, trying to make it come out even. It's like going to a bucket and always finding it full and running over! No matter how much you use, there's always more than enough left. That's the way our love for you is."

Father rumpled Tim's hair. "Now that you're the big brother, I guess we will have to treat you like an older boy. I think there had better be a bigger allowance for you. And we can count on you to take a turn at looking after Baby Sam. It's great having a helper around that we can trust."

"I think I'll buy Baby Sam a present," said Tim. "I'll buy him a little baseball. I'll keep it for him till he gets big enough to throw it. Then I'll teach him how."

"Let's go out and have a game of catch," said Father. "We'll have to keep you in

practice so you'll be ready for Baby Sam when he's big enough to play."

This is the prayer Tim's father prayed that night when Tim went to bed.

Dear God, thank you
for our son Tim.
Thank you
for making him part of our family.
Thank you for
our new Baby Sam.
Help us to make him welcome,
and care for him in our family.
Teach us to love each other
in your way of love. Thank you
for sending Jesus to teach us
and show us that there is never an end

to how much love people have
for each other,
because God's love is always
more than enough for us all.
Amen.

Gertrude Ann Priester

God Is Always Ready

Ashley squirmed around on the hard little chair in the doctor's office. There were big people in all the big chairs. Every time one of them left to go in to see Dr. King, another one came in the door! There was never a comfortable chair for Ashley!

"I'm tired of waiting, Mother," she said. "Why can't it be my turn now? We were here before those two boys that went in."

"I'm sorry it is taking so long, dear," Mother said. "Those boys needed something special that couldn't wait, so Dr. King had to take time to see them before he sees the rest of us out here. All the others had appointments before ours. Dr. King must have been kept at the hospital later than usual, and so he was not able to start work here on time."

Later that afternoon Mother and Ashley went to the supermarket. They bought some bread and peanut butter, some fruits and vegetables, some cookies and juices, and some paper napkins and soap. They had a cart full of groceries when they went to the checkout place. There

was a long line of people, all waiting to check out their purchases too.

Ashley stood on one foot, then on the other. “I’m tired of waiting, Mother,” she said. “Why can’t it be our turn now?”

At the dinner table that evening, Father was serving the juicy roast beef that Mother had cooked: a piece for Grandmother, a piece for Mother, then some little pieces for Baby Mark. “I’m tired of waiting, Father,” said Ashley. “Why can’t it be my turn now?”

When it was bedtime, Ashley’s mother came to tuck her in. “Did you say your prayers, dear?” she asked.

Ashley yawned. “Yes, I did. I could hardly keep awake long enough to say them, but I did. Mother, I’m glad I don’t have to wait in line to pray to God!”

Mother smiled. "God is always ready to listen to his people when they pray to him," she said. "In fact, God is waiting for us to come to him. He never keeps us waiting."

Dear God,
thank you
for wanting us to love you
and come to you with our prayers.
Thank you
for not making us wait for our turn.
Sometimes we forget to thank you,
or to tell you about our troubles.
Thank you
for not going away,
but waiting for us to come back.
Amen.

Gertrude Ann Priester

Don't Forget

Near a village in India an elephant had just finished his bath. Then he filled his trunk with the dirtiest water he could find in the river and went down the road to the open window of a tailor's shop. SWOOSH! He blew the muddy water all over the

tailor! The elephant had not forgotten that the tailor had poked a sharp needle in his trunk when the elephant had playfully put his trunk in the open window a few days before. The elephant didn't like that and he didn't forget the pain.

Do you ever forget? Maybe you intended to do your homework last night, but a friend came to play. Or maybe a good TV program came on and you forgot all about the lessons you planned to do. Sometimes children forget things parents ask them to do, such as hanging up clothes, feeding the dog or cat, or taking out the trash. Did you need to be reminded to do a chore today?

There is another reminder that all of us need. "Remember your Creator." Remember to tell God that you love him. Remem-

ber to thank God for all the blessings he has given you. Remember to thank God for making you and for sending Jesus to save you from your sins. Remember! Now is a good time to remember your Creator.

Remember your Creator
in the days of your youth.
Ecclesiastes 12:1

William C. Hendricks, adapted

Emily's New Home

Emily watched the big blue moving van back carefully out of the driveway and start down the street. She watched until it was out of sight, away down at the end of the street. It was a nice enough street,

but it was much different from the one Emily had lived on out in California.

Emily hugged her Sara doll close. "I wish we were at home," said Emily. "I *do* wish we were at home instead of here."

"Who's making wishes?" asked Father as he came around the corner of the house and gave Emily a hug. "Let's have some lemonade. What color cup do you want, Em?"

"Where's the lemonade? The refrigerator isn't working yet. I'll have a green cup, please," said Emily.

"Yes, ma'am," said Father. "Step right this way for lemonade in a green cup!" Father took Emily's hand and up the front steps they went. Inside in the hallway there was a big pitcher, some pretty paper cups, and a plate of cookies.

Soon everyone was drinking the cool lemonade and munching on the cookies. "They are from Mrs. King, our neighbor next door," said Mother.

"She doesn't know us yet," said Emily.

"Well, not exactly," said Mother. "But we're neighbors, she knows that! She is going to be a good neighbor."

Just then one of the men from the office where Emily's father would be working knocked at the door. "Hello," he said. "My wife, Margy, wants you all to come over and eat a picnic in our backyard. Don't bother to change your clothes. I know how much work there is to getting settled in a new house. Come on over any time you want to, and we'll eat when you get there."

Emily watched him go down the walk and get into his car.

"How do we know where to go?" she asked. "How did he know we were here?"

Father explained that his company had told the office people when he would be coming and when he would start to work. "I met Mr. Clayton, the man who was here, at a meeting not long ago. When he knew we would be moving into this neighborhood, he said he would keep his eye out for us. I guess he did!"

The next day another neighbor from

across the street came over to meet the new family. "Won't you bring Emily over to splash in our wading pool?" she said. "It is right there in the corner of the yard, and you can look across the street and see your house all the time you are playing." Just across the street wasn't far! Soon Emily was splashing and shouting with Kari and Eric, just as though they were friends! Why, they *were* friends! She stayed for a sandwich and chocolate milk, and promised to walk to school with Kari in a week or so when school began.

That evening Father said, "We are all going to take time off from fixing up our house. We are going to find out where to get a bus, where to get on the subway, and where some of the stores are."

The next day the family did just that.

Before very long they began to get "the feel of the place," as Father put it. "Cities and towns are sort of like people. You have to get to know them before you can decide whether or not you like them. I like this one."

"I like this one too," said Emily. "There's a zoo we can go to someday. The man in the subway ticket booth said it wasn't far away."

"I have some leaflets that tell about all sorts of places to go and things to see," said Mother. "We will take them home and decide which ones we want to see and then we can plan some trips. I want to get acquainted with my new city too."

That night Emily was tired so she climbed into bed early. The curtains were not up at her windows. All the toys were

not on the shelves. But she had Sara doll, and Mother and Father were here, and she had new friends, and she was getting acquainted with her city—it was beginning to feel like home!

Thank you, dear God,
that you never leave us,
even when we move from one place
to another.
Thank you that
we are never lost from you.
Thank you for good neighbors,
and for parents who show us love
and who take care of us
even when we are in new and
strange places.
Thank you for interesting places to go
and new things to see.
Thank you, God, for your love.
Amen.

Gertrude Ann Priester

Growing Up

Suzie woke up, stretched her legs under the blankets, and looked out at the bright sunshine. At first she had to *try* to think about what was so special about this day, for she wasn't quite awake yet! But all of a sudden she *was* awake! "It's

my birthday!" She said aloud. "Today's my birthday!"

Suzie jumped out of bed, raced to the bathroom, and back to her room. She pulled off her pajama top, and started to pull her tee shirt on over her head. It wouldn't come! She pulled and tugged, and pulled some more. But her arms just stuck up like a scarecrow's, and she could not get them through the place where arms should go. She looked down and saw another tee shirt lying on her bed. Quickly she shook off the first shirt and pulled on the other. It went on just the way a tee shirt should!

Suzie continued to dress, but a funny thing happened. The first of every piece of clothing she tried to put on just would

not fit! It was too small! What was going on here?

Even Suzie's shoes were too small—the first pair, that is! Right beside them was another pair—the ones she had taken off last night, she was sure of that!

Suzie ran down the stairs and into the kitchen for breakfast.

"Happy birthday, dear," said Mother.

Just as Suzie started to tell about the terrible time she had trying to get dressed, she looked down at the table. There where she usually sat were two plates, two glasses, two sets of silverware. One was the kind she always used, and the other was small and looked like baby dishes! On each plate was a small box, wrapped in bright colored paper, tied with ribbon, and holding a card that said "SUSAN."

Mother pretended to be very busy at the stove cooking the eggs. But Suzie knew that she was watching out of the corner of her eye, and she was smiling her sort-of-secret smile! Suzie decided to open the box on the baby plate first—maybe it was a trick! Carefully she unwrapped the box,

took off the lid, and unwrapped another package that she found inside.

"Oh, Mother!" she shrieked. There in the wrappings was the first little wristwatch she had received when she was five years old! It had hands that moved, a tick-tick-tick that sounded when you wound it, and a picture of Mickey Mouse in the middle of the watch face. It looked like a "real" watch! And it was what she had wanted more than anything else—when she was five.

Quickly, but very carefully, Suzie unwrapped the second box. There she found another wristwatch . . . but this was "real" one. It was exactly like her big sister Laurel's, and one that had a second hand and wouldn't stop if she happened to forget to take it off when she went

swimming! It was exactly what she wanted more than anything else on this birthday!

Mother began to laugh, and Suzie laughed too. "You did all that business with the clothes!" she said. "You put out all those little ones that I couldn't get into, Mother. Why did you do that?"

"Birthdays are great days, Suzie," she said. "Daddy and I tried to think of some way to remind you that this birthday marks a new step you have taken in growing up. We decided that this would do it!"

"It did," said Suzie. "That's for sure!"

When Father came down to breakfast, everyone had another good laugh. Suzie showed her parents and then her big sister, Laurel, how she had tried to get into her "little-girl clothes."

Then Father asked Suzie to think about some other ways she had grown up too—like being able to walk to school alone, knowing what to do when she forgot to take her lunch, remembering that Mother depended on her to look after Baby Jeremy when Suzie was left alone to watch him.

Father turned to a verse in the Bible and asked Suzie to read it. "Stop and consider the wondrous works of God," read Suzie.

"You are one of the most wondrous of those wondrous works," said Father. "That's why Mother and I played this trick—to make you stop and think! Growing up is one of God's best gifts to his children, and we should take time to think about it once in a while. A birthday is the best time I know for doing that!"

Dear God, thank you for birthdays.
Thank you that we grow
in many ways—
some that we can see

and some that we can feel.
Thank you that we can grow
in ways of thinking
and acting toward ourselves
and others.
Thank you for the special love that
people
show us
on this day,
for presents,
and cards,
and birthday cakes,
and all the fun we have.
Help us to remember
that growing up
makes people expect more of us.
Thank you that you expect more
of us too,
and that you will help us to grow
to be the persons we know we can be.
Amen.

Gertrude Ann Priester, adapted

You and Others

How Do I Show My Love for Jesus?

If someone were to ask you, "Do you love Jesus?" you would answer, "Yes, of course, I love Jesus."

But if you were asked, "How can you show me that you love Jesus?" what would you answer?

One little boy wished Jesus would come to visit him in his home. The boy said he wished Jesus would be about the same size as he was, and just as old—which was five. The boy would let Jesus sit in his own little rocking chair. They would have chocolate milk and cookies together. Then they would play together. And the boy would let Jesus have any toy he wished. Jesus could be first in any game. And before Jesus left, the boy would let him choose any toy he wanted to take home for his very own.

As the boy sat thinking, he said, "I know Jesus can't come to me as a boy my size, but I could show my love for him by letting Mark sit in my rocking chair. I could share my toys with Sam and Dan. I could let Kim be first when we play my new

game. Maybe I should let Mike choose one of my toys for his very own. He doesn't have any toys to play with."

So how can you show your love for Jesus? Begin in your own home. Don't fight with your brothers and sisters. Try sharing what you have and what you are with those around you.

Be kind . . . to one another.
Ephesians 4:32

Dena Korfker

Wrong Friends

Let me tell you a story about a boy named Alex. His mother was a Christian and she had taught him that good children obey their parents and are kind to others. One day Alex found a new friend named Chris. Chris was not a good boy. When he called on the phone to ask Alex to come to his

house to play, Alex's mother was not ready to say yes.

"He does many things I do not want you ever to do," she said. "I am afraid that if you play with him too often, you will soon be doing them too."

"Oh, Mother," Alex said, "Chris is okay, and he's my friend. We won't do anything wrong."

So, after that promise, Alex's mother let him play with Chris.

Chris soon coaxed Alex to help him catch his neighbor's cat. Chris planned to drown the cat and then lay it on the lady's porch. They couldn't catch the cat but they did trample the neighbor's flowers. And when Chris saw his plan wasn't going to work, he became so angry that he picked up a stone and broke her window.

Alex was not very happy about going home that afternoon. He knew his mother had been right. He told her what happened. He was very sorry for what he had done. His mother said Alex's punishment would be that he could not play with any friends for two days. And then Alex asked his neighbor lady to forgive him, and he asked God to forgive him too. That night Alex and his father fixed the broken window.

Alex found out that it is not a good idea to be with a boy or girl who has bad ideas and wants to get you to do wrong things. Good ideas and good friends make happy play times.

Show me your ways, O Lord,
teach me your paths.
Psalm 25:4

Dena Korfker, adapted

Quills or Kindness

Porcupines are interesting animals. They eat mostly small plants and tree bark for food. They grow to be about three feet long and are able to climb trees easily because of their sharp claws.

But the most unusual thing about a por-

cupine is its quills. Some people thought that a porcupine could shoot its quills at its enemies, but this is not so. The porcupine will slap his enemies with his strong tail. And when he does, the sharp, barbed quills are driven into the enemy. If anything comes to attack him, the porcupine can roll up into a ball and no one will want to touch him for fear of being stuck with a quill.

Not very many people want a porcupine for a pet or even want to be near one.

Some people are like porcupines. They seem to get angry easily and hurt everyone who comes near them. They may use sharp words or mean tricks as their quills. No one likes to be near them because anyone who tries to be friendly ends up getting hurt.

Don't behave like a porcupine. Don't use hard shoves or mean looks or sharp words. Ask God to help you to be kind and gentle.

Live a life of love.
Ephesians 5:2

William C. Hendricks, adapted

Real Friends

Jamie and Dave were friends—real friends! Sometimes they got angry with each other, but it never took long to straighten things out. “We can’t waste time staying mad!” said Dave. “We have too many things we like to do together.”

There was only one thing they *couldn't* do together. Jamie could not ride a bike. He tried once and fell off. He tried again and hurt his leg. He tried again—another spill! When people began to laugh at him, he stopped trying. "Let's do something else," he said.

Day after day, when the other boys were riding bikes, Jamie would look at the bikes on his front porch. He would kick at the tires and turn the handlebars. Sometimes he would try to ride, when no one was watching. But he just could not ride a bike! Then one day Jamie decided that he would ride a bike if it was the last thing he ever did! His big brother saw the look on Jamie's face that meant "I will!"

"I'll help you, Jamie," he said, and went along beside the bike to steady it. At first it seemed as though the same thing that had happened every other time would happen again. Jamie fell off once . . . twice . . . three times. But each time he got back on the bike and tried again. Just when his brother and all his friends thought for sure that he would give up, Jamie rode

for half a block without falling off! His brother shouted and jumped up in the air.

"Try it again!" said Jamie's brother, and Jamie did. This time he rode a whole block! Then he rode farther and farther, until he was riding and not falling off even once! It was a wobbly trip, and he did not go very fast, but he was riding.

While this was going on, Dave was riding his own new bike up and down another street. "I'll stay away so he won't think I'm watching," said Dave. "It feels funny to have people watching you make mistakes."

When Dave saw Jamie going around the block for the second time, he started after him on his own bike. It was a sleek, fast, well-balanced bike, and Jamie looked at it—then down at his own smaller, clumsy

one. Dave looked too. Suddenly he said, “Here, Jamie. Try my bike. I’ll bet it’s even easier to ride.”

The boys traded bikes, and Jamie started off. Faster and faster he rode. He could hardly believe his own eyes! A little while ago he couldn’t ride at all. Now he was riding as fast as Dave! Up and down the street and around the corner! All the time Dave was trying to keep up on Jamie’s clumsy old bike.

The next day after school both boys hurried home to get their bikes. Jamie was on Dave’s bike and Dave rode Jamie’s. Both boys looked so happy that people smiled at them as they raced by.

That night, as Dave was going to bed, he said to his father, “Did you see Jamie riding a bike today? It was really great!

He can ride as well as anybody now. He feels so good he can hardly stand it!"

"I thought it was your bike he was riding," said Father. "Your new bike that you wouldn't lend anyone!"

Dave grinned and looked down at his shoes. "Yeah! It *was* my bike. But you know, Dad, when he finally found that he could ride, I just wanted him to have the fun of a real ride! That old bike of his was

too little and too heavy to go very fast! I have to work like crazy just to make it go slowly. So I thought how he would feel flying along on mine . . . and I just wanted him to have that feeling! He deserved something special, he worked so hard to learn to ride."

Dear God,
help us to find ways
to show our love for our friends.
Teach us the joy of giving up
something very precious to us
when it helps a friend.
Thank you
most of all that Jesus was willing
to give up his life for us
so that we can know
how great your love is for us.
Amen.

Gertrude Ann Priester

You and God

HO
BIBL

God Takes Care of Us

God loves us very much. He showed his great love by giving his dear Son, Jesus, to die for us. Surely, if he loves us so much, he will always take care of us, won't he?

The Bible says that he will. The Bible tells us that no matter what happens, God

is taking care of us. Day and night, every day and all night, he watches over us.

Do you remember David, the shepherd boy who became a great king? David loved

God. And David knew that God loved him. David wrote many psalms, or songs. Some of them are in the Bible. One of his songs is called the Shepherd Psalm.

When David was a shepherd boy, he took good care of his sheep. He found grass for

them to eat. He led them to good clean water, so they could drink. When the sun shone hot, he found a shady place for them to rest. And he always watched. He watched to see that the little lambs did not fall off the high rocks, or get hurt in some other way. He watched to make sure that a bear or a lion did not catch one of the sheep. Before it was dark, he gathered all the sheep into the fold, the big sheep-house. There they were safe and

warm. Then David lay down in the doorway, so that nothing could get in to harm the sheep at night. David was a very good shepherd. He would even give his life if something came to get the sheep.

When David thought how he took care of his sheep, he thought of God, how he takes care of his sheep. And so he wrote a psalm, or song, about the Lord taking care of his sheep. David knew he was one of the Lord's sheep. And he knew the Lord was a good shepherd. Find David's psalm in your Bible. It is Psalm 23 in the Book of Psalms.

One day Jesus said to his disciples, "I am the good shepherd."

The Lord Jesus is a very good shepherd, a very special shepherd. He watches over

us all the time, and he never even goes to sleep!

Who are Jesus' sheep? Do you know?

All God's people are Jesus' sheep. Jesus takes care of them, just as David took care of his sheep. Boys and girls are Jesus' lambs. He loves them. He watches over them, just as David watched over the lambs in his flock. God loves us. He takes care of us.

When we remember that he loves us, we can be happy even when we are sick. We can be happy in time of trouble. We can be happy when it is time for us to die and go to heaven. There we will see our Good Shepherd.

Marian Schoolland

The Best Food

Do you love to eat? Many people have tried to set records for eating the most food at once. Philip Yazdizk ate 77 hamburgers at one meal. Thirteen-year-old Paul Hughes ate 39 peanut butter and jelly sandwiches. Other people try to see how

fast they can eat. Steven Nel ate 50 1/2 bananas in ten minutes. Sian David with his team of three men ate 100 yards of spaghetti in 53 seconds.

Good food and enough food are real blessings. We pray for this in the Lord's Prayer when we say, "Give us this day our daily bread."

The food we eat keeps us alive and well and makes it possible for us to grow strong bodies. But the Bible teaches that "man cannot live on bread alone" (Matthew 4:4).

thank you God
for Everything
SPINACH

We need to know more and more about Jesus, too. When we believe that every word the Bible says about Jesus is true, then pray to Jesus, talk to him, and listen carefully for him to talk to us, we are having the best food to grow into strong Christians.

Then Jesus declared,
"I am the bread of life.
He who comes to me
will never go hungry."
John 6:35

William C. Hendricks, adapted

Happy as a Lark

Have you ever seen or heard a lark? A lark is no bigger than a sparrow. But when he flies, he is a sight to behold! He swoops and darts and soars high into the sky. This is why he is often called a skylark. And as he flies, he sends down to you

his beautiful song! His tiny throat fairly bursts with melody. Your whole world seems filled with the sound of his singing. And you go on your way with a happy heart.

There is something which brings even more happiness to the hearts of people than the song of a bird. It is the singing of people. I think God must love music very much. He sort of built it right into his children when he made them. One of the first things a baby learns to do is to hum little sounds. And by the time a child is two or three years old, he or she is already making up little songs and singing some of the songs sung by mother or an older brother or sister.

As children grow up, they soon learn that singing is a wonderful way to show

what they feel. God is very happy when he hears his children praising him. He likes to hear his children singing. A long time ago David and some other people wrote 150 songs which they called psalms. Whenever something special happened, these people wrote a song about it.

Are you as happy as a lark? Then sing—sing now before you go to sleep. Sing with your mother or father or brother or sister, whoever is reading this story to you. Do you make your home a happy place by singing?

I will sing to the LORD all my life.
Psalm 104:33

Dena Korfker

Don't Forget the Stamp

Before you mail a letter you must address it; that is, you need to write on the envelop the name of the person who is to get the letter and where he or she lives. The name should be written clearly. The house number, street, city, and state must be

given. Even the zip code should be included.

But letters still need something else—a stamp. The money you pay for the stamp pays the cost of delivering the letter.

Our prayers are almost like letters. They must be addressed to the right person. Jesus taught us to pray to our Father who is in heaven. We send our messages to him because he hears and can answer our prayers.

But our prayers must have a stamp—the stamp of Jesus Christ. He has paid the cost. For his sake God hears and answers the prayers we send to him.

If we would pray in our own name, our prayers would not be delivered. They would be like the envelops that are never

delivered. Always end your prayers with the words, "in Jesus' name."

You may ask me for anything
in my name,
and I will do it.
John 14:14

William C. Hendricks

A Happy Birthday

"When you have a birthday, how does your family celebrate it?" asked Miss Baker, smiling at her Sunday school class.

Brian's hand was up first. "My mother makes my favorite kind of meal—you know, like hamburgers and french fries.

Besides, she bakes me a cake and puts candles on it. Then everyone sings 'Happy Birthday' to me before I blow out the candles."

"We always decorate a chair with bows of pretty ribbon," explained Katie. "Whoever has a birthday sits on the birthday chair. We put our gifts on the table in front of the birthday chair. And after we've eaten, the gifts are opened so everyone can see them. Then Dad prays especially for the one whose birthday it is."

"At our house," said Tim, "We each do or make something for the one who has a birthday. On my birthday my big brother made me a special box for my collection of stones. My mother let me choose what I would like her to cook for dinner. And

Dad took me to the zoo 'cause he knew how much I like to go."

One after the other the children told how their families celebrated their birthdays. Then Miss Baker asked, "But why do your parents and brothers and sisters do all these things on your birthdays?"

"That's easy," answered Zack, "They want to make us happy."

Miss Baker nodded. "That's right, Zack. Because they love us they want to give us joy on our birthday. On Christmas God's family celebrates the most important birthday in the world—Jesus' birthday. And because we love him we want to make him happy too. How do you think we can make him happy on his birthday?"

The children thought quietly for a few moments. "I know," said Sara. "We can all

sing 'Happy Birthday' to him. He would hear us and be glad."

"I think it would make him happy if we would tell him we love him," suggested Katie. "And if we would show we mean it by doing what he likes us to do."

"We could thank him 'specially for being born so he could grow up and die for our sins," said Tim.

"How about if we give some of our money to help the missionaries tell people about him?" asked Brian.

"Very good, boys and girls," agreed Miss Baker, looking pleased. "Do you remember the Bible verse that tells us another way to make Jesus happy on his birthday and other days too? . . . I am thinking of a verse we learned last month." Seven rememberers thought hard. But none could think which verse Miss Baker meant.

Jesus said, "'Whatever you did for one of the least of these brothers of mine, you did for me.'" In this verse Jesus is saying, "Whatever you do to make the poorest or smallest of my children glad I will count it as if you have done it for me. When you are kind to one of my children, you are being kind to me." You see, if we visit one

of his sick or sad children, or if we give food, clothing, or furniture to one of his poor children, it is as if we have done this to him.

"Since Christmas is Jesus' birthday, we who love him should not be busy thinking about what makes us happy. But we should think about him and plan to do what will please him."

Velma Kiefer

Going Anywhere?

Two men planned to travel to another city by train. But they didn't wait for the conductor to tell them where to go, or when to get on the train. They thought they could take care of themselves. They saw several cars of the train waiting on the

tracks. So they went into one, found a comfortable seat, and were soon busy talking.

After a while the conductor looked in and said, “You had better move into the car ahead.”

But the men answered, “Why, what’s wrong with this car?”

“Nothing,” said the conductor, “but it isn’t hooked onto anything that will take you anywhere. This car needs an engine to pull it!”

It takes power to move a train along the tracks. All the cars must be hooked to a strong engine.

People need to be connected to someone who has power to get them on their way through this life to heaven.

You know who that powerful one is. It is

Jesus. Jesus said, "I am the gate; whoever enters through me will be saved." Learn who Jesus is and what he has done for you. Believe that he died for you on the cross. Let Jesus live in you.

Dena Korfker, adapted

You and God's World

God Made All Things Good

Did you see something awesome today?

If you really looked around, you must have seen something awesome. There are many, many wonderful, awesome things all around us. The big round world that

we live in is awesome. The big blue sky over our heads is awesome.

Sometimes white clouds sail in the blue sky, like ships. The clouds are awesome too. They are made of tiny drops of water that sail in the wind.

At night the beautiful stars sparkle high above us—thousands and thousands of them.

There are beautiful flowers and trees.

There are bright butterflies. There are all kinds of ants that build anthills or make homes deep under the ground. There are furry animals that live in the woods, rabbits and squirrels and chipmunks. There are birds that sing and fly and make wonderful nests.

Oh, the world is a wonderful place!

Where did the world, and all these awesome things, come from?

Do you know where they came from?

Have you learned from the Bible that God made all things? He made them long ago, "in the beginning."

Before that beginning, long ago, there was no sky. There was no big round world. There were no clouds, no trees, no birds, no flowers. There were no people.

But God was there. He is the I AM, you know. He has always been. And one day he began to make the wonderful things we see.

First God made the heaven and the earth, the sky that is above us and the big round world we live on.

But the sky was dark. The world was all dark too.

Then God said, "Let there be light!" And there was light.

God is light. He made light in the world

so that we could know him and could see and enjoy the beautiful things he was going to make.

He made the oceans and lakes and rivers. He sent some of the water up in the sky, to be clouds.

He made mountains and hills. He made trees and grass and flowers. He made little birds and big elephants. He just spoke a word, and there they were!

And everything he made was very good.

God made you too.

God is awesome!

In the beginning
God created
the heavens and the earth.
Genesis 1:1

Marian Schoolland, adapted

Colors Are Great

What if everything in your home were a dull gray? What if your family room had dull gray walls and furniture, gray curtains, and gray carpeting? How would that make you feel? Not very cheerful.

Colors play a big part in our day. Soft

greens make us feel cool and restful. Bright new spring-greens make us feel alive and full of pep. They make us think of the coming alive again of all God's creation. Yellow spreads cheer and makes us feel happy.

God must have loved blue—he gave us so much of it! All the lakes and rivers and oceans look blue. And what about that endless blue sky? Blue is a beautiful color. Think about a baby's blue eyes.

Then there is brown—so rich, so soft, and sometimes so good to eat! Who doesn't like a bowl of rich, chocolate ice cream! Don't forget black—it is soft and rich and beautiful. And it makes the other colors look so much brighter.

Think about the color purple. When we mix bright red and bright blue paint

together, we get a rich purple. Purple makes us think of a window in church, or maybe you have a purple shirt or blouse.

Do you like the color orange? It is so bright and cheerful, and it helps make food look interesting and good to eat.

Then there is red—the brightest color of all. Fire engines are red. So are apples and strawberries. And sometimes boots are red. Red also makes us think of life itself, because our blood is red.

God is a God of beauty. When he planned this great world, he included color. He gave us a whole rainbow of brilliant colors!

Thank God for colors.

Dena Korfker, adapted

Jump

What do you know about frogs? Have you ever collected frog eggs or watched them hatch into tadpoles? Soon their tails drop off and they learn to jump instead of swim.

All their lives frogs are good jumpers.

It's not easy to catch a frog. Just when you think you've got one—whoops! he jumps away. And then he seems to watch you with one eye closed to see what your next move will be. But all the time he's ready to jump the split second he thinks he will be in danger. Frogs must always watch for trouble. They cannot take a nap while they sun themselves on a lily pad. Some-

one or something might catch them while they're sleeping. God gave frogs strong, long legs so they could protect themselves from danger by jumping.

What protection from danger did God give us? Well, to keep us from doing wrong things, God gave us a conscience—a little warning voice that tells us not to do something bad.

We should be more like a frog, always alert to danger. Sometimes if we see or do only a little sin, we don't notice it too much. We may repeat that sin with only a little warning from our conscience. We just are not alert. Soon we begin to like that sin and, what's worse, we aren't even bothered by more sins and bigger sins that slowly creep into our lives. Then we don't even want to be alert. And just like

a frog that isn't alert, we are going to get into a lot of trouble.

Listen to your conscience and jump away from sin. Ask God to help you stay away from even little sins and to forgive the wrong things you have done today.

Create in me a pure heart, O God.
Psalm 51:10

William C. Hendricks, adapted

Night

Are you glad that God made the night? Are you glad that every day is divided into daytime and nighttime? Sometimes, when you're having a lot of fun, you wish night would never come, don't you? But if you had to stay up all day and all night

without resting, you would soon know how wise God was in giving us the night.

In its own way, the night can be as beautiful as the day. On a clear night, the sky is one of God's great wonders in his creation. The millions of stars look like tiny diamonds sparkling on a black velvet dress. The Milky Way

looks like a long, long road that stretches straight to the throne of God. Ask your mom or dad to help you find it. And when the moon shines, the whole dark world seems to glow and sparkle. Have you ever walked in your own backyard when it was turned into a fairyland by a full moon shining on a newly fallen snow? The night is truly beautiful.

But most of the time you don't see what is going on in the night, do you? You are fast asleep in bed. Going to bed is one of the happiest times of the day. It is the time when Mom and Dad take time out to be with you alone. They read to you or tell you stories. They pray with you. It is

the time when God comes very close to his children. And when you are left alone, what do you think about? Remember all the good things that happened during the day. Plan something you could do tomorrow to make someone happy.

Sing a song to show your love to Jesus before you fall asleep. Then it will truly be a *good night.*

By day the
LORD directs his
love,
at night his
song is with me.
Psalm 42:8

Dena Korfker

BEDTIME